# GETTING OVER THE RAINBOW

my journey from self-doubt to self-love

**MATT CORKER**

illustrations by emma segal

to:

love,

share the book. spread the love.

# A LOOK INSIDE

# THIS IS MY THANK YOU

It took me 12 years to come out of the closet.
Five years to understand how I identified sexually and seven years to build up the guts to actually stand behind the words, "I'm gay."

However, it took three more years after I came out to really love myself for it. To understand how it made me who I am. To see how it aligned with my faith. And to truly understand how being gay contributed towards the legacy I was making in this world.

I tell you this so you know where I am coming from when writing this.
Five years of debate, curiosity, and confusion.
Seven years of inner conflict, experimentation, and "whoops that didn't work." Three years of tough conversations, self discovery, and generosity. And many more years to put it all into practice.

The support I felt from those around me during these years was the game changing piece of my journey. My friends were generous with their time, their lives, their dinner invites, and, most importantly, their love. Their honest words and unconditional support meant more to me in that moment than they probably knew.

**I love you.**
**I'll be there for you.**
**Oh, that's normal.**
**That will happen again if you don't change something.**

They showed up when they didn't know I needed them to. They said what I needed to hear even when it was tough to say it. They were the people I leaned on for reassurance and guidance.

They were - and still are - my biggest fans.

This book belongs to them. It is my thank you.
This book also belongs to you. So that you can be that person who one day hears that man in your life say "I'm so happy. I love my life. And I have you to thank for that."

# TO THE BIGGEST FANS OUT THERE

Biggest fans stand for our true, most authentic selves.
They want us to be happy, healthy, and successful… and able to take a good nudge in the gut when we are not being any of those.

Biggest fans remind us when we are not doing or being our best.
They are there for us in the dark days, in the overwhelmingly amazing days, in the days we hope to never repeat, and those we wish would never end.
They celebrate with us and cry beside us.

They may be miles away, yet they always feel nearby.

They remind us what it means to laugh, to love, to work our butt off for something, and to get back up after we fall flat on our face - in front of everyone. They are there to help dust us off. They remind us of our highest potential.

They are moms and dads.
They are sisters and brothers.
They are classmates and teammates.
They are best friends and avid readers.
They are teachers, mentors, extended family members, coaches, and confidants.

This book was written for them.
So that they can see themselves as a biggest fan and, in turn, be one for that gay man in their life.

This book was also written for that gay man.
So that he can be his own biggest fan and, in turn, be one to those he has in his life.

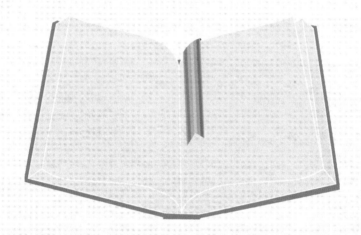

we'll read from the same
pages in this book, so
we can be just that.

on the same page.

# JUMP IN

This book is not a story. It is a jumping off point.

It is a collection of conversation starters grounded in my journey to today. It is intended to stir emotions and thoughts within you so that you'll feel drawn to engage others in a dialogue about what you've read or what you've experienced in your own life. It may even help you articulate your opinion more clearly or hear someone else's in return.

We will talk about love and friendship.
Dating and sex.
Gender roles and spirituality.
Parenting and community.
And the incredible tapestry that they weave together called life.

At the end of each section you will find a page dedicated to reflecting on your own journey. There will be questions to answer either alone or with someone you love. You will also find mini-assignments on that page designed to help you take the next step along your path. Take them, and yourself, lightly. They are intended to be both fun and provocative.

I also think it is important to acknowledge that this is my opinion. One point of view. They are written through my perspective  and experience of the world. They are my honest lens intended to shed light on topics and ideas that are much richer and more vibrant than can be captured in a one-way dialogue a book like this creates. It is not the answer or the rulebook - as no two journeys are identical. That being said, I do hope it spurs you to find your own truth along your own journey. I hope this provides light along the way.

So maybe you jump around this book - flipping from page to page in no particular order. Maybe you dive in deep - reading it from front to back. Maybe you finish this book and choose to write one of your own to fill in all the gaps. Maybe you pass this book along to someone you think should read it.

Whatever option you choose, jump in. The water is mighty fine!

# IDENTITY

how I see myself is how I see the world.

# MY CHOICE

Our lives are the result of the series of choices we make.
Something happens and we choose what to say, do, or think about it.
The different possible responses are the options we have.

When he cuts me off in traffic, I can choose to get angry, to slow down and
let him in, or I can choose to turn up the music and ignore it. When she
gives me a grade on a test, I can choose to be happy about it, to consider
it an inaccurate grade and ask for a retake, or I can choose to make that
teacher feel wrong and bad for ever giving me that grade.

Every situation presents me with options to choose from.
Each option also comes with a corresponding outcome or consequence.
Sometimes the corresponding outcome we associate with an option is so
undesirable that we don't even consider it to be an option. This limits our
experience of the choice we actually have.

For example, when planning a trip to New York, there are many options.
Multiple airlines, flight connections, and travel times can take me from
Vancouver to New York. I then apply a filter to narrow down the options
based on travel date and price. I find that the ideal flight time is out of my
price range, so I cross that off my list of options. The cost of that option is
too high. The majority of the remaining flights in my price range have too
many connections and layovers for my liking - leaving "only one option" for
me to choose.

Just like airlines, life doesn't always give us everything we want. We have to
create options for ourselves. The important thing to note is that we eliminate
the options for ourselves, not the airlines. We run each option through a set
of criteria and analyze the consequences in a way that limits our perception
of the choice we have available to us.

Sometimes we even go as far as blaming others for removing our options.
"Why doesn't the airline offer me this exact flight that I want?" However, we
always have the ability to generate new options at any time.

We always have the option of driving instead.

# IT'S YOUR CHOICE

There are some things in this life that I didn't consciously choose for myself.

I didn't choose where I was born.
I didn't choose my biological parents or siblings.
I didn't choose my eye colour or hair colour.
I didn't choose my need for glasses.
I didn't choose my wardrobe when I was a kid (and have the pictures of me in neon outfits to prove it).
I didn't choose my elementary school.
I didn't choose to be gay.

Those things were required, granted, or gifted to me.

I did however need to accept these things in order to change the relationship I had with them.

I had to consciously choose them.

I chose to love my parents and siblings.
I chose to dye my hair to see what looked good.
I chose to get glasses, then contacts, and then laser eye surgery so that I could read the chalkboard and participate in sports without worrying about something breaking or falling out.
I chose to enjoy school and the mandatory "first day photo" my mom would take every year.
I chose to love every part of me that made me me - including being gay.

So is being gay a choice? No.
Is accepting yourself as a gay man a choice? Yes.

# WHO I *SHOULD* BE

Society has created a heteronormative expectation for us to live in to. That is to say that there are social roles and structures in place that reinforce the idea that heterosexuality is the norm and that it is superior to other sexualities.

In this context, we are expected to act a certain way as a male.
We are expected to flirt or date a certain way - and only with women of course. We are expected to wear certain clothes or participate in certain activities in order to prove our masculinity. As if there was a societal test to give us a passing or failing grade on our manhood. And we are expected to play by the rules of that game.

By playing by those rules, we create what some may call a default future.

In their book *The Three Laws of Performance*, Dave Logan and Steve Zaffron describe a default future as "a foreseeable future that will occur almost for certain unless something unexpected happens."

In a heteronormative society, heterosexuality is considered what is expected while homosexuality is something unexpected.

When I am aware of what my default future is, I can either choose to live that out or do something unexpected. I can ask myself whether my default future is *actually* the future that I want to occur.

Rather than living my life by who I *should be*, I consider who I *could be* instead.

# WOULD YOU WANT TO BE STRAIGHT?

When considering who we could be one night, I asked that question to a group of gay friends I had over for dinner.

**"If you had the option of becoming straight tomorrow, would you take it?"**

One friend quickly spoke up with an adamant NO! and went on to explain his rationale, which went something like this...

In today's society, there are boxes that limit what a straight man can or can't do, or can and can't be. This is a simplified example of what is referred to as "gender roles." When he steps out of those boxes, he is considered to be unmanly or feminine.

As a gay man, society expects us to be both a man and be feminine. And, by doing so, we actually get more boxes to play in.

Society expects gay men to love romantic comedies, have a great fashion sense, and enjoy dancing. If a straight man were to like those things, his sexuality may be questioned - as strange as that may sound to some of us.

As men, however, gay men can also enjoy things like camping, watching the football game with the guys, and pumping iron at the gym without being met with the same suspicion. We aren't as confined as straight men when it comes to publicly liking what we like or being who we are.

Think about ballet dancers, soldiers, hairdressers, construction workers, or presidents. Most of those occupations come with a stereotypical gender attached to them. And since we get to frolic in the limbo between the masculine and the feminine, all become options for us to pursue.

I had never before considered that my sexuality could actually expand my options. And I like where that thought pattern will lead me.

# LOVING MYSELF IS MY CHOICE

I have a sunken in chest.
Or *pectus excavatum* to be exact.
My rib cage goes in slightly creating a concave look to the centre of my
chest.
Growing up, I was incredibly self conscious about this.
No - I was flat out embarrassed by it.

I tried to hide it.
I'd wear a t-shirt when swimming with people I'd never met before.
At summer camp, I'd choose all the activities that didn't require me to be
shirtless. I always wanted my team to be shirts and not skins.
I also dreaded taking off my shirt near someone out of fear they would reject
me.

Because of my disdain towards my chest, I limited myself. Limited the
activities I would partake in, and limited my level of comfort I felt with those
around me. It wasn't until I got tired of missing out on things I enjoyed doing
- like swimming with my friends at a birthday party - that I made the shift.

When I chose to love my chest I was choosing to live a life I really enjoyed.
A life that made me happy. A life that was easy.
No more excuses. No more hiding.
I was able to just be me.

A similar sequence of events happened for me and my sexual identity. I
tried to hide it. I dreaded when I was placed in an environment where my
attraction to men would be noticeable. I limited myself and the comfort I felt
around others.

When I chose to accept myself as a gay man, I chose a life that made me
happy.
A life that was free from excuses and hiding.
A life where I was able to just be me.
And love it.

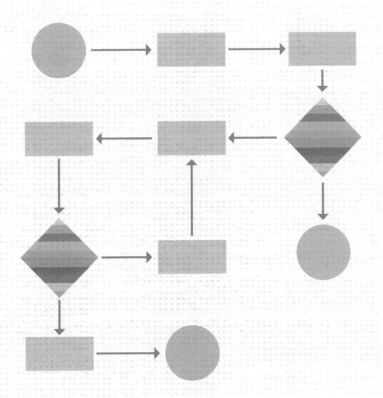

life is the result of the series
of choices we make everyday.

# WE ALL HAVE MULTIPLE IDENTITIES

We create an identity for ourselves in our career - in how we make our money; sales consultant, banker, painter, radio host, fundraiser, educator, author, IT technician.

We create an identity in our relationships - in how we interact with others; brother, grandmother, best friend, mentor, acquaintance, colleague.

We also have a sexual identity that allows us to enjoy our romantic and sexual lives; gay, straight, asexual, lesbian, bisexual, queer, pansexual, two-spirited.

We are multidimensional beings.

All these identities, and more, contribute to who we are as a person.

Our work is in integrating our identities in a way that serves us and the world.

To create ease and comfort when transitioning between situations and locations in which one identity may be more recognized than the others.

It is through our authenticity with ourselves and those around us that we are able to refine our skills, get connected to the right people, and love our life.

# YOU <u>DO</u> EXIST

Some of us may consider that some identities just simply don't go together.

CEO - mother - lesbian
Competitive dancer - grandfather - straight
Pastor - mentor - gay

I thought that once too. Until I met him.

I was living in Copenhagen at the time and swimming on a gay swim team called The Copenhagen Mermates. It was a great way to stay in shape and integrate myself into the gay community in Copenhagen at the same time.

We went out for dinner following practice one night and I sat across from one of the older members on the team. We exchanged witty banter and then I asked what he did for work.

"I'm a pastor," he replied.

It was as if I just met Santa Claus.
I'd been told my whole life that he didn't exist.
That what he did wasn't possible.
And then, there he was, in the flesh, doing everything people said he couldn't (or shouldn't) be doing.

I looked across the table at him with wide eyes and said to myself, "You DO exist!"

We find the proof we need to support what we believe to be true.
When we think identities don't go together, we find evidence that they don't.
When we consider that they do go together, we find the role models and support we are looking for.

what identities are you hanging
on to that aren't you?

- lauren phelan -

# EVERYTHING CHANGES

All good things come to an end.
All bad things come to an end as well.
Everything we experience in this life is temporary.

The relationship we have with our parents.
The number of gay men we hang out with.
How many dates we go on.
The industries we work in.
How much money we make.
The towns that we live in.
Where we go to have fun on a Friday night.
What we rely on our parents for.

All of these things will be the way they are for a season.
And then they will change.

We can actively choose to make them change - actively choosing a different default future - or we can let them live out their natural season.

When we hold on too tight to how our life is today, we don't leave room for it to grow, to change, or to transform. We try to keep our life the same and then get frustrated or disappointed when things change.

When we loosen our grip, we acknowledge that everything in our lives will change.

We can then start developing a new comfort level with change so that when life does change, we can navigate the uncertainty with ease and confidence.

# a moment of clarity

## reflect

→ What five things do you love about yourself?

→ How comfortable do you feel in your own body? Why is that?

→ How do you currently identify sexually? Who do you want to sleep with? Who do you actually sleep with? What do you tell people?

→ What expectations do you have for yourself?

→ What expectations do you feel others have of you?

→ How do external factors like culture, religion, nationality, community, or occupation influence your identity?

## action

1) On a blank sheet of paper, list out the different personal, professional, and sexual roles or identities that you have randomly on the page. Then begin to connect the identities by drawing a straight line between identities you feel go together - or are expressed together in your life. Notice which identities feel the most connected, or integrated, into your life and which ones aren't.

2) Write out three things you aren't supposed to or allowed to do (e.g. run outside naked, scream in class, quit your job, take the car for the weekend). Now do those three things on paper - write it out step by step, draw it out (stick figures make beautiful art), or make it a collage from images you cut up from your magazines. Notice how you feel when you see the final product.

i)_____

_____

_____

ii)_____

_____

_____

iii)_____

_____

_____

3) Create three different imaginary lives for you to live and write out what they would be like. Consider what your life could be like if anything were possible or if you had made different choices in the past. Consider that everything can change here and dream really really really big. Which imaginary life most appeals to you? Why?

i)_____

_____

_____

_____

_____

_____

ii)_____

_____

_____

_____

_____

_____

iii)_____

_____

_____

_____

_____

_____

4) Write out your default future - the expected future you will have if you kept everything as it is now. Where will you end up in ten years? Is this the future you want? If not, what do you want your future to be in ten years? Write that out in full detail.

**DEFAULT FUTURE:**

_____

_____

_____

_____

_____

_____

_____

_____

_____

_____

**DESIRED FUTURE:**

_____

_____

_____

_____

_____

_____

_____

_____

_____

_____

5) After you feel inspired by your ten year future, write out one thing you can do this week to help make that future possible.

_____

_____

_____

_____

_____

_____

_____

_____

_____

_____

_____

# COMING OUT

freedom is being who I really am.

# WHEN DID YOU FIRST KNOW?

Do you know you're a teacher when you get a full-time teaching job?
Or when you get a part-time teacher-on-call position?
Or when you enter a program that certifies teachers to work?
Or when you have the epiphany that your calling and passion and life mission is to be a teacher?

Our identities grow and strengthen over time because we align our actions and choices around them. They all start with the epiphany.

The epiphany around our sexual identity may happen when we first see a naked body, either in real life or through the media. It may be when we first touch someone who we like more than a friend. It may even be evident through the fantasy we create when hormones rush through our bodies as we masterbate.

For me, it was at age nine. I was going through the Sears Christmas Catalog looking for a new Lego set I wanted to ask Santa for. I flipped through the catalog and landed on the lingerie section. I started to comb the pages of bras and thongs until I came across the mens section. I became intrigued. My interest triggered a response as I studied the male physique. I was more interested in the male models than the women.

What I didn't know at that moment was what it all meant. What was the significance, if any, of the biological responses I felt when flipping through that catalog?

The teenager that has a love of mentoring and presenting information to those around them may not know in that moment that their career identity is a teacher. Though they can't deny the feelings and sensations they get when they are teaching.

We may not be able to make sense of our identity when the epiphany comes, but we sure can't deny it when it does.

# 7 YEARS IN THE CLOSET

I was ten years old when one of my best friends in the theatre company I performed in came out of the closet. He was 13. Being in the performing arts world meant that we knew and were friends with a lot of gay men - yet he was the first of my close friends to come out.

Hanging out with him and his older high school friends on the weekends, however, gave me a look into the "gay world" of Toronto. I reflected on my own sexuality at that point and realized I was gay. I told this to my mom (who cried) and my sister (who was nonchalant about it all). I then proceeded to sneak into gay clubs underage across the Greater Toronto Area (my Mom hated this), see his friends hooking up with new guys every night (I hated this), and was offered drugs I didn't even know existed (I never took any). I began to second guess my sexuality because of the type of people I was exposed to. These were not the people I wanted to surround myself with. I didn't see any role models or any relationships I wanted to emulate. Something didn't feel right to me.

So I, the kid who believed in the power of choice, chose to go back to dating girls. At the time, I thought my sexuality was something I could choose too. Spoiler alert: it wasn't.

So I fell in love with a girl, got my heart broken, became really cold and robotic when it came to the idea of love, and closed myself off from any romantic relationships. I also distanced myself from the gay community I met in Toronto. With some people, I even pretended like we had never met before. "Who are you again?" I blocked it all out.

Fast forward to my first year of university in Vancouver, where I chose to date again. I dated a girl who lived in the same on-campus residence as me.

Later that school year, my friend from the theatre company came out to visit me while both my roommate and my girlfriend were away. (You can tell where this is going, right?) In one night I became the person I never wanted to be: a cheater.
I felt horrible.

At my rowing practice the next morning, my coach made some comment about going back to our boyfriends in bed after practice as we weren't pulling like 'men.' I felt like he was speaking right to me. I felt so exposed. I broke it off with my girlfriend when she got back with no good reason - I was too embarrassed to tell the truth. I quickly found myself in a toxic relationship with another guy in the residence and my self-worth began to crumble. He would talk poorly about me in public to hide his own sexuality and then proceed to kiss me behind closed doors.

I felt like I was being used for my body.

I felt worthless.

I felt like this gay thing was all wrong ... so I retreated again.

The next year I dated an amazing girl and was completely distant in our relationship. I still felt incomplete with my last gross relationship and brought that in to this one. Dating someone when feeling used and worthless is not recommended. That old saying of "you need to love yourself before you can love someone else," is not just fluff.

By not being honest with myself, I put my girlfriend in a position to question whether our relationship being less than amazing was her fault. It wasn't, but she didn't know that at the time. She asked for some space when we broke up three months later - and so did some of my closest friends. They sensed something was "off," as if I was hiding something from them. Man, were they right. I didn't want to risk putting any more strain on those friendships though, so I chose to hide my attraction to guys once again. I chose to go back into the closet.

A year later, after the dust had settled and my friendships were all in tact, including one with that ex-girlfriend, I met a guy who liked to paint. I was so intrigued by him and we started dating. He was the first guy I loved and who loved me back. About 2 months in to our relationship, I was getting ready to meet my sister for brunch. I was in such a hurry that I just grabbed the nearest shoes; which turned out to be his, not mine.

Over brunch my sister and I caught up like we always did. She noticed my shoes as I went to the bathroom and when I came back asked me where I got them from. I told her, "They are my boyfriend's."

A smile washed across her face as she asked, "And are you happy?"
I replied yes.

In that moment, I realized that I could live a life as a *happy* gay man. That romantic love *could* exist in my world. That, while being gay wasn't a choice, lying, cheating, and surrounding myself with people that don't build me up was.

This moment was a milestone in my coming out process.
There was no more retreating after that.
I was out.

This wasn't the moment when everyone knew I was gay the very next day. This also wasn't the moment when I made sense of how my future was going to unfold while remaining true to my beliefs and values. It was simply a moment of true happiness. The start of my authentic expression; a commitment to being and doing what I say; of being able to express and receive big, juicy, heart-exploding love.

Coming out of the closet transformed my life.

# STAYING IN THE CLOSET USED TO BE EASY

Hiding my sexuality was the easy thing to do growing up.
I felt that if I kept who I was attracted to a secret, I would fit in.
I would keep my job.
More people would like me.
I wouldn't have to fear for my safety.
My family would still love me.
I would be alright.

As I grew older, hiding my sexuality became harder. I wanted to be in
a relationship - and hiding that other person in my life became difficult.
It became difficult not to talk about love authentically with my friends and
family. It was difficult having conversations about my future life with my
biggest fans.

I wanted people to like me, but I wasn't being honest with them.
I wanted to fit in, but wasn't being clear on who I wanted to really fit in with.

A level of tension and discomfort was created between what I thought
hiding would provide me and what it actually did.
'Who I was' was no longer 'who I was portraying myself as.'

Coming out allowed me to reconcile that.
It allowed me to be the person I knew I was with the people around me.
It allowed my true self to shine through.
It allowed me to see that I am worth being fully self-expressed.

# WE ARE WHO WE'VE BEEN WAITING FOR

I wanted to know what would make the transition of coming out easier, so I asked some great gay men in my life what they wish they had or what they wish they knew when they were younger. The most common responses were:

**I wish I had more peers.**
**I wish I knew there were others like me.**

In one of his podcasts, Dan Savage references three "layers" to sexual identity:
1) who we want to sleep with,
2) who we actually sleep with, and
3) what we tell other people

The responses I collected reminded me about the importance of integrating all three of those layers and of the impact that the third layer had on the larger community.

I considered that when I tell people how I identify, it allows others to do the same. That when I share with others that I identify as gay, I also allow others to feel comfortable and safe enough to also share how they identify.
In that moment, I become who I was waiting for.
Who we were all waiting for.
We become that peer we always wanted to know.

However, being the first at anything can be scary. It is the position people both glorify and vilify - be it in sport, business, or social movements. It can be lonely being first. And by coming out first, we may feel isolated at times or question whether it was the right thing to do.

This is where biggest fans become invaluable. They remind us to trust our truth. They remind us that, regardless of how difficult the road ahead may be or how alone it may feel being the first, we will be paving the way for others to travel upon.

let your true self out to play.

# COMING OUT CHANGES EVERYTHING

Who I vote for.
Who I sleep with.
Where I go on Friday night.
How I meet my partners.
Who I hang out with.
Who I marry.
How I have kids.
Where I travel to.
What part of myself I can donate.
What I save my money for.
What I talk to my parents about.
What my parents talk to me about.
How I prepare to have sex.
How I practice my faith.
What communities I join.
Who I hold hands with.
How happy I am.

Coming out changes a lot.
And, at the end of the day, it's completely worth it.

# "I'M THE SAME PERSON I WAS BEFORE."

False.

We're not the same people we were when we were in the closet.

Being "in the closet" is code for "not sharing the entirety of who I really am."

We didn't lie to people.

Well, some of us may have.
Instead, many of us hid the truth.

So people got to know the person that was slightly less than our true selves.

Heck, we were still discovering who our true selves were.
They knew and loved 80% of who we are. Maybe 95%. Maybe 57%.

However, anything less than 100% is not 100%.

So when we choose to be our full self, when we choose to be fully expressed in all areas of our lives, and when we choose to share our sexual orientation with others, we take one more step in becoming 100%.

And that is different than us at 80%.
So we have changed.
Slightly.

"You've changed" is a compliment, not an attack.

# STILL FRIENDS WITH THE EX

Who I was in my relationships with girls was my version of 80%.
By not sharing who I fully was, I held back in these relationships.
I guarded my heart just as much as I guarded my true identity.

Today, I am still incredible friends with the last girl I dated.
She remains one of the only exes I am still amazing friends with - of either sex.

While she initially felt used and mad after we broke up, like many do following the conclusion of any relationship, the space we gave each other allowed us both to see how much we still valued the other person.
We began hanging out again and that was great.
When I told her I was gay, her first response was relief.

It was reassurance that our relationship not working out had absolutely nothing to do with her as a person. Her answer to "why didn't he like me" was finally answered. The suspicions she had during our relationship were validated.

Coming out also allowed me to be 100% with her. I was able to see how our relationship was a stepping stone in the right direction on my journey, not a barricade that ever held me back. I was able to acknowledge her for the role she played in creating that greater clarity of who I am.

Who I am with her today is different than who I was in our relationship.
The jerk she dated is not the friend she has now.

And while I may not have been the best boyfriend to her, I am so committed to being one of her great friends. I'm blessed in the fact that she shares in that commitment too - not all exes do.

It may have taken years, but I am so glad we can now both look back and poke fun at "that one time we dated."

# "I ALREADY KNOW"

Boy those words stung.
Growing up, with a lack of positive role models or friends that were gay, the only gay people I regularly saw were those I didn't want to be anything like. I saw them on the 9 o'clock news after being beaten outside a gay bar or invited on talk shows to share how to accessorize the latest fall fashions.

That wasn't me.
That wasn't the identity I wanted for myself.

After I told my friends that I was gay, I hated hearing "I already knew that." It was as if they saw in me all the qualities I didn't want to be stereotyped as. I was so committed to defining my gayness on my own terms - not by some stranger they saw in the media.

And now things are different.

Now the media shows families, award winners, social activists, political figures, teens in schools, primetime TV hosts, and business executives that are gay. There are positive role models out there that are getting more air time than they did when I was growing up.

And the trend is continuing in a positive direction. Heck, you can now read a "list of gay, lesbian, or bisexual people" that is being curated on Wikipedia.

Their sexuality is part of the conversation now. And what that means is that there are now great gay roles models in the public eye that I can identify with. Who I would be proud to be like.

So when you hear "I already knew you were gay," I invite you to consider that they see this same greatness in you.

# LIVING IN THE SPOTLIGHT

Bloggers, celebrities, talk show hosts, news anchors, teachers, pastors, politicians.

If we chose to live or work in the public eye, I believe we have a responsibility to be honest with the public. And like any other figure with fame or a strong public reputation, people will want to know about who we are. They will want to know what goes on behind the curtain, the camera, or the written words on the screen. They want to get to know us by knowing about our personal lives.

This desire to get to know us may be experienced as a little invasive. It not only impacts our own life, it impacts the lives of those we choose to spend time with.
Our friends, our families, our partners.
It is our responsibility to let those we care about know how our public reputation may impact the relationship we have with them. Do they want their life on display just like us?

Being honest with the public also means being honest about our sexuality. Whether we want to be or not, we are gay role models. As Rick Mercer, a well known gay Canadian journalist, states in one of his rants about the increasing numbers of gay teen suicide "The problem is, adults, we don't need role models. Kids do. So if you're gay and you're in public life, I'm sorry, you don't need to run around with a pride flag and bore the hell out of everyone, but you can't be invisible. Not anymore."

And this may cause some of us to counter that with thoughts like:

**But what if I lose my job?**
**But my profession has nothing to do with my sexuality?**
**But I don't want to be known as the "gay one."**

All of those are valid concerns.

I also believe that if the public asks about our life or makes a comment about our assumed girlfriend - as a gay role model, we have the responsibility to correct them.

We have the opportunity to tell the truth.

We have the opportunity to tell the truth about who we are and what we stand for.

**Actually, I'm gay.**
**Actually, he's my boyfriend.**
**Actually, I'm not ok with using that derogatory term.**

While some of us may not want to make a huge statement about being gay to the general public, that does not negate our responsibility to correct false assumptions or comments.

It does not negate our responsibility to tell the truth.

# "I THINK YOU'RE GAY"

I once met a guy that I noticed some stereotypical gay qualities in.
Yet he didn't tell me he was gay.
He didn't talk about his relationships and, when he do, he used feminine or gender-neutral pronouns.

I forget in those moments that he could have actually identified as bisexual or was with a person who didn't identify with one particular gender. But I suspected that he was hiding something because I knew what he was like when he was telling the truth and when he was lying.

Sidenote: we may think we are good at hiding our inauthenticity.
Newsflash - we're not.

And yet I still didn't know what I needed to do to let him know that I was ok with his sexuality and that I felt comfortable talking about it with him if he wanted to. I wanted to be his friend in this after all.

In this case, I continued to be a loving person who showed interest in his life and supported him in what he chose to do. I remained a safe space for him and other queer people I knew. I did this because it was something I believed was important and I considered that how I treat others may signal how I am going to treat him as well. He can then determine, in his own time, that he can trust me and that he can tell me how he identifies in terms of his sexuality.

This process may take months.
In this case, it took years.

Good thing biggest fans are known for their patience.

sometimes I'm waiting for you to
ask the question because then I know
you're ready for the answer.

# A NEW BATCH OF FIRSTS

My first second glance from that cutie at the coffee shop.
My first love note from a boy.
The first queer person I meet.
The first time I get butterflies when he holds my hand.
The first time he kisses me.
The first time I kiss him.
Our first date.
Our first dance.
Our first fight.
Our first time.
Our first time using toys.
Our first home.

My first experience at a gay bar.
My first routine sexual health check up.
My first queer film festival.
My first one night stand.
My first gay wedding.
The first time I feel discriminated against because of my sexuality.
My first rally.
The first time I watch gay porn.
The first time I get caught watching gay porn.
My first gay best friend.

The first time I hear a song blatantly promoting equality on the radio.
The first openly gay President of the United States or Prime Minister of
Canada.

There are a lot of firsts to look forward to as a gay male. They will teach you
something new about yourself or about the world.

Welcome each as a new beginning.

# "THEY COME OUT SO YOUNG NOW."

I look at kids today who are beginning their journey at such a young age and I am simply amazed. They are coming out in elementary and high school and I find myself asking the question:

**How do they know who they are at such a young age?**

And then I hear the same question directed to me by the gay men that are my father's age that may have only come out in the past few years. They grew up in a different time and are filled with just as much wonder about me as I am about today's teens. I also remember that I began entertaining gay thoughts when I was nine, and I just didn't know what to think of them or have the courage to ask questions about it.

When I see a kid come out at a young age today, I honestly breathe a sigh of relief.

Thank God these kids won't break as many women's hearts as I did. That they won't get married to a woman and have kids with her and then get a divorce when they come out. That they can be leaders in a movement of social change longer than I can be.

That they will learn about tenacity, friendship, and self-respect before they hit higher education or the working world (where those are all needed in spades).

These thoughts don't make the choices my generation or generations before mine made wrong or less valuable. To me they validate that this generation will have the ability to learn from our actions and choose to do what serves them.

On the other hand, these kids are also entering into a world where they may be a target of discrimination earlier than I was.

For that reason, I see these youth as incredibly courageous. They are doing something I was too scared to do when I was their age. They are engaging in important and difficult conversations that their predecessors may not have been comfortable having.  And I am so excited to see what kind of leaders this will make them.

I'm excited to be part of a world run by those kinds of leaders. They've got my vote.

# a moment of clarity

## reflect

→ When did you first know about your sexual identity? Was there an exact moment or a general trend over time?

→ What are the benefits to you coming out of the closet? What are your hesitations to do so?

→ Who would you want to be the first person you tell about your sexuality? Who was the first person you told about your sexuality? Why?

→ Who haven't you told about your sexuality that you want to tell? What is the payoff of not telling them? Is the payoff worth it?

→ Who are gay role models that you admire or respect? Why?

## action

1) Coming out to someone is a conversation. For important conversations like these it may be a good idea to practice with another person. Ask someone you love who already knows about your sexuality to role play the person you want to have the conversation with - they play your sister or your boss and you practice how you will tell them what you want to tell them. You can even invite your role-playing partner to ask all the questions you expect to hear to then feel prepared with your answers to them.

2) List out five things that make you feel confident, loved, or connected. A favourite song. An article of clothing. A photograph. A quote or passage from a book. A best friend. Consider having those with you or easily accessible when having the coming out conversation.

i)_____

_____

_____

ii)_____
_____
_____

iii)_____
_____
_____

iv)_____
_____
_____

v)_____
_____
_____

3) Go into your actual closet and take out three outfits that don't represent who you are today. Donate or gift these outfits away. (It's nice to get things out of the closet, right?)

# COMMUNITY

when I surround myself with people that believe
in me, everything becomes possible.

# I'M OVER BEING ALONE

If I kept myself isolated, I would remain isolated.

No offer to help or exciting proposition would change things if I kept choosing to be isolated.

When I choose to be part of a community, things shift.

I begin to seek out others that are like me.
I take a risk and sign up for that gay sports league.
I say yes to that party invite.
I reach out and ask for help.

And what I seek becomes what I find.
Camaraderie.
A listening ear.
A fun night out.
Real friends.
A sense of belonging.

It exists.

It is also up to me to choose it.

# WHEN I NEED MY BIGGEST FANS

When I fail the test.
When I get dumped.
When I am too drunk to drive home.
When I land my dream job.
When I say yes to the man that makes my heart sing.
When I don't know where I am and I feel alone.
When I need some help financially.
When I get into a car accident.
When I break-up with the man that used to make my heart sing.
When I sign up for a race that feels big.
When I receive an award.
When I don't get the promotion I thought I really deserved.
When I get a diagnosis that scares me.
When I get accepted into that program.
When I lose it all.
When I decide to quit.
When I choose to stick with the challenge.
When I come out to someone that I care about.

I need my biggest fans when I am faced with character-building situations.

I call on them for non-judgemental advice and counsel I can trust.
I also call on them for the shoulder to cry on or to plan the evening out to celebrate it all.

In order for me to receive the love and support I am looking for from my biggest fans, I first need to invite them into my life and tell them what is really going on.

# WE CAN'T ALWAYS DO IT ALONE

The majority of the success I've experienced in my life has been a result of the support I received when I asked for help.

It first requires me to be clear on what I want though: a job at that company I love, a great score on that important test, a date with that cute boy from the coffee shop.

I then have to actually ask people for help. *gulp*
For those of us that sometimes struggle in finding the right words to ask for help in a powerful way, try:

**Hi <insert name here>.**
**I need your help.**
**What I need your help on is...**

Sometimes I ask the wrong people for help not knowing, at the time, that they were the wrong people. These are the people that will say things like "you're not good enough Matt," "you'll never be able to do that," or "he'll never be into a guy like you." These things don't serve me or my big goals.

When I do find the right person, I immediately know it. They are generous with their knowledge and advice. They are honest and provide me with the real facts. They are also uplifting - leaving me more motivated or committed to my goals than when I first started to talk to them. They help me take the next step towards that big dream - or first date.

I remember this whenever I think I need to "do it alone."

Surrounding myself with the right people makes each success sweeter - and, in some cases, even more possible.

choose to see the
world with love.

# THERE'S PLENTY OF FISH(ERMEN) IN THE SEA

Pretend for a second that you get really excited about fly fishing. You love the time in the water, finding the perfect bait, and the struggle it is to reel in a big one. You could go on for days about how great fly fishing is.

Now also consider that who you're currently surrounded by are not really keen about fly fishing. Or at least none as much as you are. That doesn't make them bad friends. It just means they don't like to fish as much as you do. They are still important friends to have as they could introduce you to their joy of cooking, of slam poetry, of kayaking, or of yoga - things you may not have had exposure to yet. They become the friends that enrich our lives.

That being said, it is still important to fuel your passion and to scratch that itch you have within you to fish.

And that may require meeting some people that love fly fishing as much as you do.

Creating a new social network can be frustrating at times. After all, it's easy and familiar to hang out with your non-fishing friends. In the long run, however, it won't serve you or your passion for fishing.

And just think of all those fly fishing junkies who are missing out on knowing who you are. Someone they would love to share their tackle box secrets with or go fishing for hours with.

There is a community of people out there who are just as passionate about what you are - waiting for you to come join the fun.

It's time for you to go fishing.

# THE EXAMPLE I ASPIRE TO BE

When I first came out, I hung out with the only other gay guys I knew at the time. They were older than me. They liked to party at places where drugs were making their rounds. And they were my first gay friends.

As time went on, I began to realize that I didn't enjoy sneaking into clubs with a fake ID or lying to my mom about who I was hanging out with. I also realized that none of these guys were the kind of people I wanted to be like when I grew up. They were not the role models or examples I was searching for at that time.

And I thought to myself "if this is what it means to be gay, then I guess I am not gay." I mistakenly associated their lifestyle with my sexuality and decided that I wanted neither.

I went back to dating girls, unsuccessfully still, until I met a group of gay guys at university. They were well-spoken, intelligent, and involved in their community. They went on wild adventures outside - climbing cliffs and surfing waves. They had a group of friends that included different genders, sexualities, and races. They laughed really loudly in the cafeteria. They had fun together.

They were the gay guys I wanted to be like.

It was easier for me to come to terms with my sexuality when I saw in someone else a glimpse of who I wanted to be.

thank you.

# MY GAGGLE OF GAYS

My best friend is straight. We've been friends for almost a decade.
He watched me struggle as I dated girls and was the first person to know about my first boyfriend. He is a rock in my life that I constantly look to for support (and fun adventures).

And there are some things we just don't talk about. How to best flirt with a boy. How best to handle those awkward moments during sex. How to bring up my preference of being the top or the bottom.

Not because it would be awkward; we just tend to talk about things we can both relate to - or things we could support each other with. And, unfortunately, he has yet to come up with the best way to pick up that cute guy across the room. (His recommendation to "just go talk to him" usually does well though.)

This is precisely where my gaggle of gays comes in. The gaggle is that group of great gay guys I am proud to call my friends who I rely on for support in life's gay-er things.

They are each from a different walk of life. In the gaggle is an architecture student, an American-Canadian who married the guy of his dreams after meeting online, a yoga instructor, a budding politician, an engineer working on urban transportation systems, a recruiter, a teacher, and an aspiring international news reporter. Each one of them brings something different to the group - be it a perspective or a life experience.

I reach out to my gaggle when the Queer Film Festival is in town, when I need some relationship advice, when a new article is written that may educate or offend our community, or when a new shirtless photo of Zac Efron is making internet headlines. They are my go-to gents for a good laugh and some tough love. They are my support system that really gets me.
We laugh together.
We debate with each other.
And ultimately have a gay 'ol time together.

(Pun intended)

# PRIDE AND PREJUDICE

Growing up, I had many questions and hesitations about my local Pride celebrations. I saw shirtless men parading around the street, drag queens hosting night time events, and local companies gay-washing their businesses by showing their immediate support for equality and gay rights. This all seemed bizarre to me because the men in feathers did not portray the gay community I felt a part of.

I felt that Pride was a misrepresentation of what being gay meant.

So I became more curious, asked more questions, and donned on my speedo to join the masses to experience it all first hand.

I asked myself "what are we supposed to be proud about anyway?"
It's not like there is a straight pride parade, so it must be more than celebrating our sexuality.
To me, Pride is a celebration of being who we are.

It is a showcase of the fact that I am proud to be me and that I don't need to be anyone but that. I am also proud of where I live and the privilege it provides me. I am proud we get to celebrate in public.
That is cause for celebration in and of itself.

And while we may not have accomplished something historically significant by simply being gay, our queer community has faced and overcome centuries of hardships and oppression from educational, political, medical, and religious institutions. We march in a parade as a reminder of their activism and the groundwork they laid for us. We march as a reminder that even being seen by the public can help them consider us as members of their community as well.

I remember feeling frustrated that who the public sees on television or on Pride advertisements didn't showcase who I was. After all, we're not all leather daddies, sparkly twinks, voluptuous drag queens, or speedo-clad muscle heads. That's true. We aren't all like that.
However our community does include fine men that are like that.
Our community is colourful and so our celebration of it will be as well.

While the "businessmen in suits" look may be attractive or feel representative for some of us, most gay men (and advertisers with sponsorship dollars) enjoy a little skin every now and then. So when the front page covering Pride quotes a young man seen in feathers and glitter, there is usually no hidden media agenda to make the gay population look ridiculous. It's usually just good copy. And, kudos to that young man for getting us on the front page in the first place!

So then why the party? Why not have a month of educational programming instead about self identity, LGBT history, and fundraisers that support local queer initiatives? I say, why can't we have both? Many societies that organize Pride are beginning to look at what other programming can take place while their community is a captive audience.

I believe we make Pride a party because then we can let everyone know they are invited too. For at least one day of the year, the crazy and not-so-crazy contingents from every walk of life can come together and wish each other a "happy Pride." It's as if "happy Pride" is our way of saying "congratulations on being you." Congratulations for enduring any hardship you faced in order to be honest with yourself and with those around you. Congratulations for showing us what self-expression can really look like.

So while Pride isn't perfect, it is still a privilege to be able to celebrate who we are and give thanks to those that have paved the way so that we could party in the street together.

To me, Pride is a perfect representation of what being gay means.

# FAGGOT

Noun.

A small bundle of sticks.
An effeminate gay man.
An insult alluding to the once common practice of burning people at the stake for suspected homosexual practices.

A term that gay men have reclaimed as their own.

If I was called a fag in the Inquisition-era, I would be burned at the stake - whether I was actually gay or not.

That slur would end my life.
That was its intended use.

Now, when I am called a fag, it is in reference to my "feminine" qualities as seen through a heteronormative lens. My masculinity is called in to question.

Sure it still stings when they spit it at me in a derogatory fashion.
And it definitely doesn't strengthen our relationship when they choose to do that.

But regardless of how flaming or feminine I may be in their eyes, it is only our connection that will be burned by those words.

# WE TEACH OTHERS HOW THEY SHOULD TREAT US

For a community that sticks together so closely, there is still a lot of hate slung around.

**He's such a slut.**
**Why doesn't he just man up and ditch the glitter.**
**What a fag.**
**That guy is way too old to be hot.**
**That twink has no idea what he's doing.**
**He is going to regret wearing that tomorrow.**
**Has that guy ever even been to a gym?**

We look for acceptance so often from other communities, yet often forget we too have work to do within our own. What if we eliminated the gender roles, heteronormative views, and derogatory slurs thrown in our own community first?

Maybe the rest of the world would follow suit.

Let's change our game if we want them to change theirs.

# "WHAT'S WITH ALL THESE OLD GUYS?"

When I was younger, I was a little weirded out by the fact that older gay men would hang out with gay guys much younger than them. They were at the same clubs, the same dinner parties, and on the same community sports team as guys half their age - if not younger.

At first I thought they were total creeps. *"Why don't you find someone your own age to hang out with?"* I'd say in my head. I saw them as predators. Past their prime. And simply out of place.

As I got older, and as I became more inquisitive about why this interaction is so common in the gay community, my perspective has shifted.

There are not as many gay men as there are straight men in most cities. We are a minority population. And, like birds flying in formation, we find strength when we move and work together as a group. A pack. A gaggle.

Our strongest members can help and support our struggling members. As I studied the interaction between old and young gay men, I realized that the gay community has such a strong sense of mentorship to it.

The "It Gets Better" campaign started by Dan Savage is such a perfect example of this. The majority of older men want to support, to help, and to build a sense of belonging for those just joining our community.

Those struggling to fit in can then benefit from the support decades of experience can provide.

They no longer need to feel alone.

And then one of my best gay friends told me he was really attracted to older men. That salt and pepper hair was a big turn on for him.

It was then when I remembered that there is that aspect to this pairing too.

# a moment of clarity

## reflect

→ Who believes in you? Name at least three people. Look hard. They exist.

→ Who do you believe in? Name at least five people.

→ Who do you consider to be your best friends? Why? What can you count on them for?

→ What are characteristics of the friends or supporters you wish to be connected with in the future?

→ What activities, events, or organizations do people with those characteris tics participate in or support?

→ What do you have to be proud of? What accomplishments, privileges, or distinctions have you created you can be proud of?
What accomplishments, privileges, or distinctions have others created for you - either directly or indirectly - that you can be proud of?

→ Which members of the queer community can you be more loving towards? What would that look like?

## action

1) List out the five friends or fans that you would want to spend eternity with.

i)_____

ii)_____

iii)_____

iv)_____

v)_____

2) Call four members of your community that you admire and share with them what you appreciate most about them. Yes, call them. They may benefit from hearing the conviction in your voice when you finish the sentence "I wanted you to know that what I appreciate most about you is…"

i) I appreciate _____ because of their _____.

ii) I appreciate _____ because of their _____.

iii) I appreciate _____ because of their _____.

iv) I appreciate _____ because of their _____.

3) Schedule in or buy tickets for three upcoming LGBT events that are distinctly different from each other. A fundraising dinner. A foam party. A lecture on a LGBT-related topic. A race hosted by a LGBT organization.

i)_____

ii)_____

iii_____

4) Say yes to two things in the next month that you know will be good for you yet may take some guts to actually go and do. Do them.

i)_____

ii)_____

5) Invite your closest friends, or a new friend you just made, over to cook a meal with you. "Too many cooks in the kitchen" is a great reminder that we're not in this alone. The outcome of this may be seriously delicious as well. Plan out your menu here:

**GROCERY LIST**

_____  _____  _____
_____  _____  _____
_____  _____  _____
_____  _____  _____
_____  _____  _____
_____  _____  _____
_____  _____  _____
_____  _____  _____
_____  _____  _____
_____  _____  _____

**DRINKS**

**APPIES**

**MAIN COURSE**

**DESSERT**

# DATING

going from hello to goodbye and experiencing everything in between.

# "I KNOW THIS OTHER GAY GUY..."

**You two would be perfect for each other. Let me introduce you.**

Whether it is said in the context of dating, friendship, or even potential business partnerships - being gay is usually not enough to make a connection work.

Sure, we can have something to talk about right off the bat. The conversation usually dies down pretty quickly if there isn't something else there to back it up.

Similar core values.
Common interests.
Complimentary habits around health or career.
Similar outlooks on life.

It's as if I would say:
**I know this other straight person...**

# ALL THE GOOD GAY MEN ARE TAKEN.

This is a view of scarcity.
As if there is not enough great guys in this world for everyone searching for one.

And, when I think this thought, I look for and notice around me all the reasons why that belief is true. I look for the proof that will make me right.

This thought, however, doesn't serve me in finding a good, available guy.
Because I don't notice them!
I only notice the ones that are not available.

What would happen if I thought that love was abundant?
That good single guys are just waiting for me to say hi to them?

How would those thoughts change my actions?
How would those thoughts change my relationship status?

love is the ultimate
renewable resource.

- eoin finn -

# "IT'S NONE OF THEIR BUSINESS WHAT I DO BEHIND CLOSED DOORS."

You're right.
They probably don't want to hear about that thing I can do with my tongue.
Or the position that makes me orgasm in no time.
Or maybe they do?

I don't want to keep it behind closed doors though. Most of them certainly don't.

What I really want people to know is who I do it with.
I want them to know who I love and who turns me on.
I want them to know who I am checking out when we go to the bar together.
I want them to know who is coming with me when they invite me to dinner.

Because I can then choose when I bring it up in conversation rather than hiding it all the time.

Integrating our identities is freeing. There is nothing to hide, no conversation that is too taboo, and no "other life" I need to worry about.

It's one life.

Whole and complete.

# AND SOMETIMES I DON'T

Sometimes I want to keep what I do or who I'm dating behind closed doors. Or at least behind a door between me and that specific person.

Maybe because they don't occur to me as someone who would accept me. Or maybe because I suspect my stories may offend them.

Maybe our culture doesn't condone these types of conversations at work or at home.

Or maybe I actually don't know how to talk about it in a way that makes me feel powerful yet.

Sometimes the conversation about sex and sexuality has its "time and place" to be fully discussed in a meaningful way.

I agree.

ask me about the person I am dating.
let me fill in their gender.

# LEARNING HOW TO SWITCH TEAMS

I used to date girls.
I genuinely cared for them and was attracted to them.
I even loved a few of them - in the big "I love you" kind of way.

I also appreciated the unspoken approval I felt by my family and friends when I was dating. It felt like I was doing something right; as if being single was wrong. I learned the rules to this dating game so I could continue feeling this sense of "rightness." I learned what a romantic date was, what a "good boyfriend" would do, and how to interact with others with my girlfriend by my side. "Hi, this is my girlfriend _____" would roll off my tongue with ease.

It became my badge of honour and my shield to hide behind. Because, at the same time, I was continuing to notice other guys. And they were noticing me. While my relationships were great, something was missing. Something was just not working. Some spark was just not there.

It was as if I was playing volleyball - a sport I loved and knew the rules to well - and something was just not clicking for me anymore. Even though it was the norm to play volleyball, it was becoming a struggle to get on to the court. Volleyball was an amazing sport and it wasn't for me anymore. Dating girls was an amazing experience and it wasn't for me anymore.

So I switched teams and began dating guys.

It was as if I put down the volleyball and picked up a basketball. I had an idea of what I was doing as I was still dating a human being, after all. We still went on dates together where I tried being that "good boyfriend" and I would still introduce him to friends and family. But how I did all of those things changed. I was on a new court, a new playing field, with different people, playing by a different set of rules.

And the crowd around me sat in a different formation around the court. Depending on where I was on the court at the time would now impact how close or how far away I was to different people in the crowd.

Like picking up a basketball for the first time, I had no clue what I was doing.
I was scared.
I was nervous.
And there was so much I didn't know nor was very good at yet. However, it felt so right that I was willing to put in the time and energy towards changing that.

By switching teams, I had to re-learn the rules of the dating game. This was an invitation to figure out how I was going to play on this court.
Where do I meet guys?
How do I ask for his number?
How do I tell if he's gay - or even into me?

Furthermore, my friends and family had become accustomed to me dating girls. They had their seat in the stands and knew all the rules of how to play volleyball. They even brought their proverbial signs to each game to show their support.

My Dad was the one to whisper in my sister's ear, *"Do you think Matt is gay?"* He was cheering me on while I played volleyball, yet sensed that basketball may be something I'd be more interested in.

That pissed me right off.
*"Dad! Can't you see that I'm playing volleyball here!"*
I wanted him to be with me where I was - to be present to what was going on in my life.

When I finally started dating guys, that required my fan club to get out of their current chairs, move to a different court, and find new chairs where they could still catch and support all the action happening on the court. That, at least, was my request. That they too make that transition and offer the same support they did before.

What I didn't consider was that some people would say no to that request. They would not change with me because they loved volleyball and they loved their current seat. It wasn't personal. It was just their preference. And because I had been with both guys and girls over the years, they may have thought that I could date girls again. That I could just "come back to volleyball" again. That wasn't going to happen as I learned that that was not how I authentically identified. And I needed to be ok that I may lose people who were once close to me when I admit that to myself. A good friend in high school, a best friend in fact, said our friendship would end if I was gay. She was going to stay on the volleyball court. And, as stated, our friendship ended when I picked up a basketball.

Friendships are different than blood lines though. I believe there is something special in a family that supports each other, regardless of which court each member plays on.

I didn't consider that I would need to help my family and friends learn the new rules of the game once they were in their new seats though. Because, just like it was new for me, this was new for them.

*No - there is no 'woman' in the relationship.*
*Yes - raising kids may be an option still.*
*No - every date doesn't need to start on the dancefloor and end in the bedroom. We exist outside of those two arenas.*

They would cheer at the wrong times sometimes.
*No - he's actually just a friend, nothing more. That's why you see us hanging out so much.*

They would also get upset over something that wasn't a foul move.
*Yes - my boyfriend is allowed to hang out with other guys be them gay or otherwise.*

They were learning.

And it was so easy to get frustrated with them. Each time I felt that urge come over me, I was reminded of the fact that they were there. They made the shift with me and were now learning the rules, the norms, and all of the things we needed to in order to be successful in this new game of life.

We were in it and able to learn these things together.

# PUBERTY: THE SEQUEL

When coming out later in life, some friends of mine report having a "second puberty." Just like when hormones were swirling around when our voices started to change, hair was beginning to grow, and when we started to smell really bad - hormones begin to dance through our bodies again when we start to act on our attraction towards men.

It's like we remember we have a penis and what it can do.

Some people choose to relieve these new desires through promiscuous sex, nights of solo masterbation, or by diving into a serious romantic relationship. Others may choose to go the exploratory route and quickly discover other aspects of the queer community - performing in drag, attending equal rights rallies, checking out the local bathhouse.

Instead of walking out of the closet, they take the slip 'n slide.

When I see a friend experiencing puberty part two, the best thing I can do for him is encourage him to be safe - with his body and with his heart. As much as he may deny it at times, his emotional heart still functions and it doesn't want to get hurt.

So I let him ride the wave of excitement.

He may calm down after riding out the rush or jump back on his board and go back out for more.

What I do know is that this surfing lesson in love may teach him something new about himself he will need later in life or may remind him of something that he values.

Something that he doesn't want to lose with the changing of the tides.

# CREATE A LIST OF NON-NEGOTIABLES

When I began dating, I had ridiculously high standards that most guys would not be able to meet. They hardly had a shot of dating me before they even said their first word to me. Where did that leave me? Single.

Some of my friends, on the other hand, chose a different extreme and dated anything with a penis. They would jump from guy to guy, taking whatever option presented itself. Where did that leave them? Lacking confidence. They didn't feel good enough for anyone.

When we came together, we realized that rather than standards we could have a list of three non-negotiables. These would be the three things a potential partner must have in order to be "boyfriend material." They were the musts, the checkboxes, and the only requirements to go on the first five dates.

This helped my friends be more discerning and not date guys that would continue to break their hearts all the time and they allowed me to loosen up a bit.

My three non-negotiables have become:
1) health conscious: he treats his body and his mind with respect - expending energy and refueling in a way that serves him.
2) faith: he has a grounded optimism that things will turn out for the best and that it truly only gets better from here.
3) sense of adventure: he can turn anything into a hilariously great experience - be it getting lost on a spontaneous road trip or trying to cook the turkey for our family Thanksgiving.

What they look like, where they live, how old they are, how much money they make, what their family life is like, what they do for work, how many guys they've been with before me, or the pick-up line they used on me … can all vary.

Align on values.
Everything else is negotiable.

# LEARNING MY LESSONS

When I needed to learn how to express my love to a guy because I was still uncomfortable doing so, I dated a creative poet who shared his sexuality with the public as beautifully as he shared his art.

When I needed to learn to let go of my desire to control my love life, I took home a guy from a wedding the night before he flew back across the country.

When I needed to find my confidence as a gay man in the public eye, I dated someone who introduced me as his "friend" and nothing more.

When I needed to get clear on my core values, I dated guys that didn't take care of their health, that lived life without goals or dreams, or that invested their money in shiny things.

I didn't know that I needed to learn those things while we were dating.
I can see now though that I always attract into my life the lesson I need to learn.

we get what we need before
we know we need it.

# THE GUYS I DATE ARE A REFLECTION OF WHO I AM

He dumped me.

And all of a sudden the sweetheart that I bragged about to my friends became the crazy idiot who I would never want to be with.

I began to reflect on how I spoke about my ex boyfriends. I noticed that all of the nice qualities that I previously highlighted in my conversations had been replaced with ones that described all of the things I didn't appreciate about him.

He was lazy.
He didn't eat well or exercise regularly.
He was addicted to his job.
He wouldn't make time for me.
He only attended events because they would boost his ego and his reputation, not because he actually wanted to go to them or because he cared about what cause the event was for.

My judgements and the language I chose to use, however, didn't reflect poorly on who *he* was. They reflected poorly on who *I* was.

Afterall, a week prior to our breakup he was a "true gentlemen," "a perfect compliment to my life," and "a passionate young professional changing his industry."

By expressing my judgements the way I did, I told the world the type of person I dated, the type of person I loved, and, ultimately, the type of person I was.

When I spoke of my ex-boyfriends like that, I was someone who dated lazy people that didn't eat well or exercise regularly. I was someone who loved ego-centric workaholics that cared more about their reputation than the people around them. I was someone other than the me I knew myself to be.

When I judge another person, I am communicating to those around me how judgemental I am. The focus shifts away from them and on to me - whether I acknowledge it or not.

So now, he dumps me - and I tell people of what a great guy he was. "He was artistic and funny and willing to go on such random adventures in the blink of an eye. And yet we didn't work out."

Because those are the type of guys I want to date.

Because that is the type of guy I am.

# SOME RULES TO DATING NEVER CHANGE

Be their biggest fan.

Be honest about where you are at with the relationship. Leading someone on doesn't feel great on either end.

If seeing them feels like a chore, its not working.

Accept everything about them.

If it hurts - stop, slow down, or use more lube.

Find the balance between routine and wild adventure - both in and out of the bedroom.

Say "I love you" when you mean it.

Forgive them.

Make a point of making them feel special.

Appreciate everything they do for you, especially the small things.

Give back.

If you want them to change, don't date them. They won't.

If you want them to stay the same, it won't last long. They will change.

Love them in their entirety.

# a moment of clarity

## reflect

→ In your opinion, what is the difference between "dating," "seeing someone," and "being in a relationship?" Which of the aforementioned, if any, are you looking for right now?

→ What can you do today to help you meet someone that may also be looking for what you are looking for?

→ What lessons have you learned from your previous relationships? (Remember, lessons teach us "what to do" and "who to be." Warnings teach us "what not to do" or "who to not be.")

→ What habits or beliefs do you have that sabotage the success of your relationships?

## action

1) List out your three non-negotiables. Come back to that list in a year to see if any have changed.

i)_____

ii)_____

iii)_____

2) Go on two dates with two different people who you'd normally say no to. Write down what you learned - about yourself, about the other person, about dating in general, etc.

**DATE #1**

Name:_____

What we did:_____

_____

_____

What I learned about myself: _____

_____

_____

**DATE #2**

Name:_____

What we did:_____

_____

_____

What I learned about myself: _____

_____

_____

3) Describe in writing the kind of romantic/sexual partnership you want right now. Do that again for the partnership you want 10 years from now.

Today I want:

_____

_____

_____

_____

_____

In 10 years I want:

_____

_____

_____

_____

_____

4) Practice saying "thank you" when someone compliments you instead of brushing it off or saying its "no big deal." Fully experience being appreciated by someone else.

5) Write down how you would describe your ex-partners to your best friend. Notice how the language choices you used to describe them actually reflect on and describe you.

**EX-PARTNER #1**

_____
_____
_____
_____
_____
_____
_____
_____
_____

**EX-PARTNER #2**

_____
_____
_____
_____
_____
_____
_____
_____
_____

**EX-PARTNER #3**

_____
_____
_____
_____
_____
_____
_____
_____
_____

6) Go on a double date with someone you trust. Ask them to give you feedback on how they perceived you on that date. It may provide an interesting perspective on your date demeanour.

What I learned:

_____
_____
_____
_____
_____
_____
_____
_____
_____
_____
_____
_____
_____
_____
_____
_____
_____
_____
_____
_____
_____
_____
_____

# PARENTS

they do the best they can.

# THEY WILL SCREW UP

So will you.

There is no instruction manual for parenting a gay child or growing up as a gay man. Every model will be built differently.

Sometimes parents will have questions that we don't know the answer to yet.

We can't always be their teacher.
We may be figuring it all out at the same time as they are.
We are students in this together.

I invite parents to get curious rather than frustrated.
To read articles and books.
To connect with other parents with gay children.
To reach out to resource centres or LGBT organizations that can offer support.
To allow themselves to make mistakes along the way.

The answers we're all looking for will reveal themselves when we are ready to listen to them.

# STOP DOING WHAT DOESN'T WORK

Showing up late to that meeting.
Lying to a friend.
Eating unhealthy foods.
Dating people I'm not ridiculously attracted to.
Saying I'll be there - and then never showing up.

Those don't work. And sometimes I expend more energy in creating new excuses or new ways to compensate for how much they don't work, instead of just not doing them.

Instead of striving to make "what doesn't work" work, I can choose to focus my energy towards making "what does work" work.

For example, I can be in a relationship that doesn't seem to be working. Maybe it's a romantic relationship or maybe it's a relationship I have with a family member.

It's not working.
And I still love them.

I can't stop being a son though.
Just like my Mom can't stop being my Mom.
We can, however, stop emailing each other once a month and start being in better communication with each other. We can also stop hiding the hard stuff from each other and start telling each other the truth about how we are feeling.

I can stop doing what doesn't serve our relationship to make room for what does.

# BUT MOM, DO I HAAAAVE TO?

I still need to clean my room.
I still need to respect my curfew.
I still need to be kind to my sister.
I still need to do my homework and eat my peas and carrots.

Just because I told my parents that I'm gay and that they may have been nervous about coming across as unaccepting, doesn't mean I got free reign to bypass our house rules.

They still applied because I was still their child living in the home they had created.

When I became an adult and created my own home with my own house rules was I then able to ask my parents to respect those. And how I run my home and how they run theirs may be very different, or remarkably similar.

That being said, there are some house rules that parents may set that limit our self expression:
**Your boyfriend is not welcome in our home.**
**You can not dress like that when you are here.**
**You are not permitted to hang out with those boys.**

These rules invite a conversation to take place. Our parents provide these rules with the best of intentions. They want what is best for us.

We can choose to let those rules stand or we can help them understand how those rules may not be what is best for us.

We can also help set new rules that still honour their intention of being a great parent.

# DID YOU REALLY JUST SAY THAT?

My Dad would ask me one question at almost every chance he could when I was growing up:

*"Who are you dating today Matt?"*

The word *today* stung.

It was as if he was calling me a promiscuous man whore who flittered around from boy to boy - tasting a new flavour on the regular. I wasn't that guy yet I still let that incongruency aggravate me.

In actuality, he knew that I wasn't that guy either.
He asked me that question because it was his way of making it ok for me to talk to him about my relationships. He wanted to make it seem like casual chit chat, even though it was still a conversation he was trying to get more comfortable with.

Parents may say things that sound offensive, uneducated, or closed-minded at times. Know that they are doing the best they can at being a parent.

Let their screw-ups and mistakes last only a moment.

Maybe then they will be able to treat yours the same way too.

# SOMETIMES PAIN IS INTENTIONAL

Sometimes parents will also choose to be offensive, uneducated, and closed-minded.

They will intentionally say or do hurtful things.
And that is their choice.

You can choose to believe their words as truth, or you can choose thoughts and actions that actually serve you. Thoughts that make you feel powerful, confident, and truly you.

You have the capacity to make that choice.

You have the capacity to be in the proverbial boxing ring and, blow by blow, stand even taller.

Let their choices be theirs - their fists, their harsh words, their hate.

Let your choices be yours - your patience, your forgiveness, your ability to respond with love.

The results generated by choices fueled by hate or resentment never seem to last as long as ones fueled by acceptance and grace anyway.

add in a little more forgivness.

# IS MY SON GAY BECAUSE I DID SOMETHING WRONG?

In actuality, my sexuality has very little to do with what my parents did. Except having sex.

Their biological matter played a large part in who I am.

That being said, their parenting definitely had an effect on my expression of my sexuality.

By telling our parents that we identify as gay, they can feel good about having brought up a man who has the courage to stand up for himself - even in the face of adversity.
Who is willing to be honest.
Who feels comfortable enough around them that he can be himself in their company.

Imagine how that courage and self-expression will manifest in other areas of our lives.

If anything, I'd argue that our parents did something so very right.

# BUT WHAT DO I TELL THE NEIGHBOURS?

Parents may consider having a gay son or brother a burden on them or their family. They may consider a gay uncle or nephew to be the "odd one out." They may also consider that he is an embarrassment or a disgrace to the family name.

By doing so, they create their son or uncle to be:
A burden. Odd. An embarrassment. A disgrace.

And deep down, I know that they actually love him. In my heart of hearts, I know that they would never want him to feel out of place, isolated, or unwanted - especially by them.

Consider that these initial thoughts are a manifestation of our parents own insecurity, of their own desire to look good and impress others. Their concern over their family's reputation may be impacting the relationships they actually have as a family. Their ego could be getting in the way of expressing the love they really want to show.

So, if you are comfortable with your parents sharing your personal information, invite your parents to tell the neighbours the facts: "my son is gay." No justification or back-pedalling is required.

Encourage your parents to give the neighbours space to draw the conclusions about you, your family, or even them as parents that they want to - be them amazingly positive or uncomfortably judgemental. Remind your parents to let your neighbours thoughts be theirs.

We can't control what other people think.
We can control, however, what we choose to think.

I invite you to choose the actions and thoughts on *your* end that demonstrate the love and connection *you* wish to have with your family. Put your relationship ahead of your reputation.
Be the example other families will one day strive to be like.

# HOW YOU VIEW PEOPLE LIKE ME MATTERS

**A menace to society.**
**Too flamboyant to be considered a real man.**
**A role model for the community.**
**A friend, like everyone else.**
**An abomination.**

We choose how we see the gay men in our lives. Sometimes we choose that viewpoint without even knowing that there is a gay man in our life.

They could be a nephew. A best friend's brother. A classmate. A client. The person who sits next to you at your reunion. That guy you say hi to at the gym. A reporter. A local karaoke star. Or even the guy who gave you this book.

How we talk about gay men at home, at school, or at the office has the opportunity to determine the quality of our relationships with gay men. It doesn't, however, determine whether we have a relationship with them or not. A relationship in some form likely already exists.

The viewpoint we choose to have about gay men can impact the quality of the relationships we have with these people. Blanket statements of love or hate are heard by the people in which those statements are about - whether we know it or not.

What I offer to you is to choose a viewpoint of love, of connection, and of curiousity. Explore what doesn't make sense before writing it off as bad. Share the love you have with strangers you haven't met yet.

You may uncover a gay man willing to converse with you about that topic you don't fully grasp or you may help someone receive the love that you so badly want them to feel.

# I'M ACTUALLY LISTENING

There are moments when I am listening more intentionally to my parents.

When they meet their first gay person.
When they see a gay man on television.
When I tell them I'm gay.
When I tell them who I'm dating.
When I introduce them to that person I'm dating.
When they explain their opinion on gay marriage or equal rights.

These are a few of the moments when I am listening so closely for their response because it gives me clues about our future.
About how they may view me.
View people like me.
Or view the people that I love.

These moments are moments of influence.

Our future may be changed for the better if they choose to respond with love or compassion.
Our future may also be changed if they choose to respond with hate or judgement.

Sometimes they forget that we are actually listening.

# I AM NOT HIM

Even though that gay guy on TV is not me and my parents' comments are not directed at me directly - I still listen personally.

I listen as if he *is* me and as if their comments were directed at me.

On one hand, this is something I can work on.

I can practice understanding that I am me and that that guy is that guy. And we are different. And what they say about him is not what they may say about me.

On the other hand, I also see the sameness in us. And how, even though he isn't me, we share many commonalities - be them values, communities, or experiences.

What they say about him, in this case, they say about me at the same time.

They can always worry about what perspective I will take about what they say.

Or they could choose to speak with love and compassion every chance they get, and then it wouldn't matter.

what if it had nothing to do with them?
what if it all became easier as soon as
you became ok with being you?

# a moment of clarity

## reflect

→ What do you appreciate most about your parents? Why?

→ How do those positive qualities, traits or behaviours show up in your own way of being?

→ What about your parents frustrates you the most? Why?

→ How do those tension-creating qualities, traits or behaviours show up in your own way of being?

→ If you were a parent, what values would you want to pass on to your children? How would you do that?

→ What can you forgive your parents for? Something they said, something they did.

## action

1) Write down what you would like your relationship with your parents to be like in five years. Share that vision with them so they know what you are working towards.

_____

_____

_____

_____

_____

_____

_____

_____

_____

_____

_____

_____

_____

_____

_____

2) Ask your parents what their relationship was like with their parents. What did they learn from them? What did they struggle with in that relationship? Doing this exercise may increase your empathy for and understanding of your parents.

_____
_____
_____
_____
_____
_____
_____
_____
_____
_____
_____
_____
_____
_____

3) Ask your parents what values they wanted to pass on to their children. Notice what values align and which differ from your list.

**MY VALUES:**

_____
_____
_____
_____
_____
_____
_____
_____
_____
_____
_____
_____

**THEIR VALUES:**

_____
_____
_____
_____
_____
_____
_____
_____
_____
_____
_____
_____

4) Ask your parents how they feel external factors like culture, religion, nationality, community, or occupation influence their identity and behaviours.

_____

_____

_____

_____

_____

_____

_____

_____

_____

_____

_____

_____

_____

5) Parents worry about their children all the time. Ask them what they worry about the most when it comes to you. Consider how you can help alleviate or reduce their concern in this area while still being authentic to yourself.

**THEIR BIGGEST CONCERNS:**          **HOW I CAN ALLEVIATE IT:**

6) Research the era in which your parents grew up, focusing on what significant LGBT events or discussions were happening at that time. Knowing the time they grew up in may allow provide more appreciation or understanding of who they are today. When my parents grew up...

_____
_____
_____
_____
_____
_____
_____
_____
_____
_____
_____
_____
_____
_____
_____
_____
_____
_____
_____
_____
_____
_____
_____
_____
_____
_____
_____
_____
_____
_____
_____
_____
_____

# ONLINE LIFE

being connected is a blessing and
sometimes not so much.

# FROM PERSONAL ADS TO MOBILE APPS

In his book "Classified: The Secret History of the Personal Column," H.G. Cocks notes that the first personal dating advertisements were posted in the 1700s by agencies looking to pair eligible bachelors with bachelorettes wanting to be married. After all, in that era, being single after 21 was seen as shameful and so "lonely heart" ads in the newspaper became seen as that last resort.

Cocks continues to explain that, "in Britain, the personal column was suspected (much like the Internet is now) of harboring all sorts of scams, perversities, and dangerous individuals. At least that is what the police tended to think, and they only stopped prosecuting lonely hearts ads in the late 1960s — until then they often thought that they were mainly placed by prostitutes and gay men." Police would prosecute the suspected gay men that used these ads because homosexuality was still illegal in Britain until 1967.

When the internet was created and later grew in popularity, people went online to place personal ads - or profiles - on newly created dating sites. In 1996, the first dating site for male-female partnerships, *Match.com*, was launched. Three years later, *Gaydar.com* came on the scene to cater to the group of men that didn't want to find a girlfriend or a wife. The era of "meeting someone online" quickly unfolded with more niche dating sites emerging to help people of specific religions, locations, sexual identities, and activities connect with each other.

When the iPhone App store and the Google Android store launched in 2008, the dating game changed once again. *Dating DNA* launched the first "dating application" you could buy through these app stores in 2009, which was actually more of a mobile extension of its already functioning website.

*Grindr*, however, which came out later that same year, was the first mobile-only application in the dating market. I also use the term "dating" loosely here. What makes this so remarkable is that, throughout history, heterosexual dating norms defined what services were available or channels were to be used for dating. *Grindr*, on the other hand, only catered to men seeking other men.

Since it leveraged mobile phones' location-based GPS capabilities, it created the era of "meeting someone nearby." And while dating services for straight people quickly created mobile apps too, it was gay dating apps that led the way this time. *GuySpy, Scruff, Hornet, Growlr, Mister, Manhunt*, and *Jack'd* all took the stage shortly after *Grindr* was released.

All this being said, a similar stigma still exists with mobile dating as did with personal ads back in the 1700s. They are sometimes seen as a last resort and filled with scams, perversities, and dangerous individuals. And while there may be some truth to that, the stigma today is about as inaccurate as it was 200 years ago.

People want to connect with each other.
Sometimes for right now and sometimes for a lifetime.

The online world may have a bad reputation in some circles, yet it serves as a great reminder that what we are looking for may be just around the corner.

# IGNORANCE IS A CHOICE

The power of Google and Wikipedia has made information available to anyone privileged enough to have an internet connection. And they have translated that information to be read in multiple different languages for multiple different countries.

Need to know what the difference between a bear and a silver fox is?
What the symptoms of gonorrhea are?
Where the nearest gay bar to your house is?
Or what significance Harvey Milk and the Castro District play in the history of LGBT people?

We can learn a number of things just by searching for them. Once we find a new factoid, we may be so intrigued that we go deeper and consider how we can best understand what this new information means, how it applies to our own lives, or how the language used to describe the topic impacts how it may be understood.

The vault is now open for us to be curious.

Your key is just a click away.

# DO YOUR HOMEWORK

| | | |
|---|---|---|
| twink | equal opportunity | kink |
| top | sixty-nine | MSM |
| open relationship | gusband | bottom |
| bear | genderqueer | ally |
| HIV | D+D free | blow |
| daddy | gender reassignment | basic rights |
| QPOC | metrosexual | gaydar |
| one night stand | dildo | homoflexible |
| lube | beard | fag hag |
| BDSM | gay for pay | trans* |
| raw sex | drag queen | positive discrimination |
| orgy | marital rights | vanilla sex |
| friends with benefits | hanky code | golden shower |
| civil union | two-spirit | cis-gender |

Joining the gay community felt like moving to a new country in
some respects.
I met different people who spoke a different language.
They knew terms and acronyms that I initially had no idea about.

While there is no Lonely Planet handbook to help navigate this new territory,
there is the internet.

I invite you to search the above terms and then ask questions to learn
more about them.

There are many more where this list came from.

Warning: some of these may be NSFW (not suitable for work).

# FIND SITES THAT BUILD YOU UP

I remember when I first started reading "gay news" on the Internet. More accurately put, I was reading "anti-gay news" on the Internet. Blogs that focused on hate crimes and discriminatory legislation. Articles that gave "evidence" for why homosexuality was wrong. Videos that villified or negatively stereotyped gay men. Like always - what I looked for, I found.

My perception of myself was influenced by what I read, watched, and listened to.

I didn't like what I was consuming though because I made it mean that I was abnormal, strange, and bad.

I realized that technology offers us another option. It allows us to connect with hubs of support and insight that can make someone feel loved, normal, and worthy.

The "It Gets Better" Project.
Glee.
YouTube channels like: Gay Family Values or Davey Wavey.
The Gay Men Project.
Hello Mr.
#instagay

And the list goes on.

When we choose to consume media and information that builds us up, we may get the courage and support we need to face that which tries to tear us down.

# I LIED TO YOU

Younger men have the option of lying about their age online to access restricted content or adult communities. Porn, dating sites, or certain mobile apps being the most common.

They may do this because they are curious.
Or they may want to learn more about something or someone.
Or they may also want to meet someone just like them.

Older men, on the other hand, may lie about their age online to avoid the ageism that still exists in some communities. In those circles, old is unavailable. Old is desperate. Old is creepy.

They may want to show others that they are not defined by the number of years they've had on this planet.

Others lie online by using good lighting or a great filter to make their six-pack seem more defined than it actually is.

Or they list activities that they aren't actually interested in, but consider them cool to have on their profile.

Some may even lie about being online in the first place - creating anonymous profiles that don't include any recognizable features about them (like their face or name).

And the result?
Liars attract liars.

Consider what could happen if we were genuinely honest online - about what we wanted, about what we did for fun, and about who we were.

Honesty, afterall, attracts honesty.

# SOMEONE LIKE YOU

Sometimes I feel totally alone.

Like no one truly, really deeply and personally, understands what I am going through.

Or what it's like to be me.

What it's like to be the one guy in the family bringing another guy home for dinner. What it's like to have a crush on a boy when all my friends are checking out girls. What it's like to be asked to be part of a blood drive at work and say "they won't accept my blood because I sleep with men."

These moments of loneliness come and go. Like waves, sometimes these feelings crash into me, and other times they slowly come in and slowly go out.

They go out when I remember that I'm not actually alone. Even if I was to isolate myself in a remote city in the middle of nowhere, there would still be people (or at least one person) who deeply cares for me. Who wants me to be overwhelmingly happy and successful. And there would also be people (or at least one person) who is just like me.

Who is feeling alone.
Who wants to meet, or even just talk to, someone they can relate to.
Someone like me.

All I need to do is reach out (or log on) and I find what I am looking for.

# I'LL MEET YOU ONLINE

Some of us live in remote destinations.
Some of us live in countries where it is unsafe, physically, to be an out gay man.
Some of us live in or near vibrant gay communities yet still don't feel like we belong there.
And some have a specific attraction to a certain type of man that we don't casually meet in our day-to-day lives.

So we go online.

We go online to talk to or meet others like us.
To remember that we aren't alone.
To relieve that sense of disconnection we feel.
To find someone to date or sleep with.
To experience what it feels like to be appreciated or noticed.
Or to help those that are looking for any of the above.

Feeling connected allows us to remember the truth that we are never truly alone.

The sun always shines even when we can't see it.

# ONE DAY YOU MAY CHOOSE TO MEET SOMEONE YOU MET ONLINE IN PERSON

At an event.
At a pub.
At a mutual friend's party.
At his place.

This is because there is no substitute for offline friends.
Friends that I can see and talk with in person on a semi-regular basis.
Friends that I can go on adventures or grab a coffee with.
Friends that I can hug.

There is something special about being in the presence of someone that cares for us as much as we do for them.

Trust your judgement when shifting from online to offline. If it feels weird - like something they've told you doesn't seem to add up - or its just a one time thing, take precautions. Have a backup plan, a friend to call, or a easy out if you need to get away quickly.

It may also feel really exciting and you may be genuinely interested in furthering a friendship or relationship with this person. In this case, search for the good in the other person when you first meet. They probably feel as uncomfortable about this as you do. Plus, few people actually enjoy spending an entire meal trying to prove they are good enough for someone else. Give them the space to relax and feel comfortable around you.

Instant judgement may work online but it doesn't translate well in real life.

# IS THIS REAL LIFE?

One day our online and offline worlds will be completely blended into one. We already see the trend of personal and professional lives combining together.
One day so will our digital and tangible spheres.

The work we get to do before that union happens in a really profound way is to create consistency between who we are online and who we are offline.

The profiles, the propositions, the pictures, and the promises that we make online will soon have an impact on our lives after we close the laptop - regardless of our privacy settings.

To some of us that is terrifying.

To others it sounds like absolute freedom.

It will be the era of real life living, not online lying.

Are you ready to live a self-expressed life as if it was always on display?

# FACING THE ONLINE HATE

Hateful words sting. When I am called names or ostracized in a digital space, it really stings. Mainly because the speaker is usually only using a status update to evaluate me as a full human being. They forget that their firey words are actually to another person just like them.

They feel comfortable doing or saying things online because they are actually afraid of doing them in person. Or they think that they should harass me both online and offline, just so I really understand how poorly they think of me.

I have taken a lot of online flak in my day and have developed pretty thick skin. I believe it is because I forgive people really easily.

I know that if they felt the pain they inflicted on me, they would choose differently.

I relate it to stepping on a beetle on the sidewalk. If I felt my own leg break when the beetle's leg broke, I would think twice about stepping on the little guy. We don't feel the direct effect of our words or our actions. I trust that, if we did, we would make different choices.

So they sling words of hate at me and I think, "would you really want to feel the way I feel when I hear those words?" and I forgive them for acting without that level of consciousness. I find I even have to offer myself that forgiveness too when I mis-speak or step on a proverbial beetle.

One time the online hate was so consistent and so hurtful that I actually said "I just want this to all be over." I realized as soon as I said that phrase that some people replace the word "this" with "my life." Some people see no other way to end the constant hate than to kill themselves. After all, it would all be over then.

So I encourage you to consider your words online. Do they add fuel to a burning fire of hate or do they offer support in putting it out? Would you want your comment to be someone's breaking point? On the other hand, would you want to let their comments stop you from living out your legacy?

everytime I stand up for myself or something
I believe in, I show others that it's possible
for them to do it too.

# a moment of clarity

## reflect

→ How do you feel about connecting with gay men online? Why is that?

→ How do you feel about meeting men through a dating website or a mobile application? Why is that?

→ What are your go-to sites you always check out when you are online? How do these sites make you feel?

→ What queer resources or communities do you enjoy checking in with online?

→ What do you do when you feel bullied online? Who could you talk to if you felt this way?

→ What do you do when you see someone else being bullied online?

## action

1) Google your name and list below what comes up first.

_____

_____

_____

_____

_____

2) Describe yourself in 30 words or less. (This could be your next online profile bio.)

_____

_____

_____

_____

_____

3) Get a friend or colleague to provide feedback on how you come across online. Give them links to your website, your dating profile, or your social media accounts so they can see what inconsistencies there may be or what great personal quality you may want to highlight more.

**THEIR FEEDBACK:**

_____
_____
_____
_____
_____
_____

4) Grab a camera, or scroll through your photo library, and select a face shot, a body shot, and a picture that shows you doing something you love. These could be the first photos you share when asked.

5) Meet up in person with three guys you met online. Notice how their profile picture or information either accurately or inaccurately represent themselves. Apply your learnings to your own online profiles.

**PERSON #1:**

_____
_____
_____
_____

**PERSON #2:**

_____
_____
_____
_____

**PERSON #3:**

_____
_____
_____
_____

# FAITH AND THE FUTURE

dark clouds only hide the sunshine.
they can't stop it from shining.

# WHERE IS THE LOVE?

Sometimes it is hard to see that there is anything good or fair about my current situation.

I get dumped.
I get left at the club by myself.
I get hate mail in my inbox.
I don't get invited to the party.
I don't have anyone to talk to about it.
I don't have someone to back me up.

These situations are like when the wifi goes down in my apartment. I am no longer in a position to connect to the source of the internet. I need to physically remove myself from my apartment and go to a coffee shop that has wifi, or log on to a device that has its own internet connection.

It's not that the internet left me, it is just that I needed to connect to it in a different way.

I needed to change something about my current situation to remind myself that I always have the ability to connect back in.

We always have the ability to reconnect back in to a place of love and acceptance.

Love is always present - we just need to change our situation sometimes to fully experience it again.

# WHAT IF TODAY WAS NOT AN ACCIDENT?

When I lived in Copenhagen, I lived with a gay Mormon. We had a number of chats together about faith, friendship, self-image and his love for airplanes and good europop.

Like our faith, our definition of "good" europop was also different.

One of the topics we would consistently come back to was *purpose* and *living life intentionally.*

In one conversation we entertained the thought:
"What if I woke up on purpose today?"

As if waking up was a cosmic call to say, "Ok Matt, you've still got work to do here. Wake up and get to it."

As if waking up was the signal that the legacy I was meant to leave on this planet hadn't been fully lived out yet.

If that were true, what would I use today for?

# IT'S NOT EITHER / OR

When I introduce myself as a gay Christian, it sometimes surprises people. They create an either/or framework and try to place me in to it.

"You are either gay *or* Christian," they say.

And that could be true for them; that I need to be one way or another. However it is not true for me.

I know this because I am both.

I am not an "either / or."
I am an "and."

I am gay *and* Christian.

Even though people try to limit who I am, I remain in the practice of not limiting myself or the possibilities I can create. I come back to what I know to be true.

"And" is my truth.

"And" allows me to live a fully expressed life.
"And" allows me to feel limitless.
"And" allows me to contribute towards my legacy.

# HIS NAME

I don't talk about God very often in my writing or my daily life. It could also be argued that, at the same time, I talk about Him in every conversation I have.

When my conversations include reference to my Highest Self, the Universe, our true nature, or Love - I am referring to Him. No these words are not synonyms for God. Yet they may be more approachable for certain people and may evoke the feeling and connection in others that I feel when I use the term God.

These words may be more approachable to individuals because we humans have juxtaposed the name of God beside words of hate and ignorance. "God hates fags" is an infamous sign a certain church in the US totes around to state their opinion of homosexuality at events or near people that support gay rights or equal opportunity. It has become an iconic phrase that some may now associate with God. That statement was not a direct quote from a biblical text though, so we can correctly assume that it was human interpretation that created it.

I don't use the term God often because I speak to, have friendships with, and am one of those fags they reference on that sign. So I try a different approach. I believe God would too.

Some of you may say that I am watering down the power of His name by not using it directly. You are correct. The sign carried by that 5-year-old member of that church also waters down the power of His name. See - we are on two sides of the same coin. We both want God to be known - and there are different approaches to that.

Love. Grace. The Universe. God.

The invitation I offer here is to be open enough to consider what each of those mean to us - and forgive those (ourselves included) that know not the fullest impact of the actions we take in helping others understand our interpretation of them.

# MY LAST TIME IN CHURCH

I previously attended a church in Vancouver with my boyfriend who also identified as a Christian. We would attend with our friends and made it part of our relationship, yet didn't make it publicly obvious that we were a couple.

I began volunteering with the church, serving on the audio-visual team during Sunday services. As the pastor became more vocal and clear about the stance that this particular church took against homosexuality, I felt conflicted. One one hand, he would praise people like me for being a serving member of the Church and, on the other hand, condemn people like me for being a homosexual.

I approached the pastor who was responsible for the volunteer program and told him that I was stepping down because I didn't believe I was the type of leader this church would want as a serving member. I was a leader who, among other great qualities, identified as gay.

He looked back at me and said,
**"Thank you for stepping down."**

My heart sank.
My preconceived notion of how this church would react to me coming out was actually true.
It was the first time I felt unwelcomed in a church.

It was also the last time.

Just like political leaders have different approaches to running their governments, different religious leaders have different approaches to running their sacred spaces. Furthermore, even leaders within the same religious denomination vary on their approach and protocol.

I say it was the last time I felt unwelcomed in a church not because I stopped attending church. It was the last time because I went online to find the churches in my district that were LGBT friendly. I also found and joined the Gay Christian Network and met a number of great gay men that share my faith.

We attended church together and developed friendships founded in the commonality of where we put God in our lives. First.

"Thank you for stepping down" will forever be a reminder that it is not God that creates the divide between humans on this Earth.

Humans create the divide.

The divine is what connects us.

# ME AND THE BIG MAN UPSTAIRS

There was one a time in history where interracial dating was taboo, weird, and downright wrong. In some communities, it still may be.

In this situation, people tell other people who they can and can't be in a relationship with. They tell them their opinion.
Some people that share that opinion may even be in a position of influence that can institutionalize this personal opinion in that community. This could force two interracial lovers to be separated from each other physically or be unable to experience the same privileges as lovers of the same race would. The love between the two people is tested in these cases.

Being a gay Christian means that my personal relationship with God may be tested because people will also tell me whether they think I can or can't be in that relationship. Their opinion, however, doesn't change our relationship status.

I go to church to learn more about my relationship. Since He knows everything about my life, I want to learn more about His. (I don't want our relationship to be one-sided after all.) Luckily sermons from around the world have been recorded and posted online as videos or podcasts for anyone to listen to. So whether I was kicked out of the church because I was not a welcomed member of their congregation or I just missed a service because I was out of town, I can still get my weekly lesson and dedicated time to focus on my relationship with God.

Prayer is always available to me as well. At the end of my yoga classes, right before I go on for a big presentation, or when I am walking by the ocean, I can have a moment of silence and tune in to His presence in my life. I do this to give thanks, to ask for help, or to pray for someone else.

So as institutionalized as someone's opinion may be about whether I can or can't have a relationship with God, I will always be able to have one.

I will always be able to believe in what I believe in.

And no opinion can ever take that choice away from me.

# WHEN IT'S NOT EXPECTED

There are certain groups of people that I expect won't accept me. They are consistent with their public stance against homosexuals and don't give me any indication that their views are changing.

Unlike my sexuality, I believe that their stance could change in the future.
Yet I am grounded in the fact that, today, that is their stance.
That doesn't mean I condone it.
It just means that that is what it is.

However, I am caught off guard when I experience hate from an individual or a group of people that I wouldn't expect it from. It surprises me.

When my uncle sits across from me at dinner and declares that homosexuality is a choice and not one he'd want for his son.
Or when my coach uses a gay slur to indicate that our team performance was less than ideal.
Or when a student gets expelled from a private high school because he came out to his class.

I am reminded that hate can enter into these safe spaces.
And, while we don't refer to it as bullying, the impacts are quite similar.

# WHY ME?

**"Why do I have to be the one to deal with this?"**
**"Why can't my life be more like his?"**

Sometimes I ask myself these questions when times get tough.
Sometimes I want to just throw my hands up in frustration and say, "I'm out!
I don't want to deal with this anymore!"

And then I consider my life 10 years from now.
What would my future self want me to do here?
What actions can I take, as difficult as they may be, to respond to my
current situation in a way that supports the legacy I want to leave? That
supports the relationships I want to nurture?

Those questions remind me that patience, forgiveness, and resiliency create
the results I would be proud to look back on.

Take actions today that your future self will look back on and thank you for.

I may not be able to deal with it all today.
that is why there is tomorrow.

# WHAT ARE YOU THE CURE FOR?

Consider that anything we overcome in this life, we become the antidote for.

When parents get divorced and your relationship with them remains amazing, you may become the antidote for split families that hate each other, or the antidote for kids who feel like it was their fault.

When you stay together for that year he moved abroad - facing all the ups and the downs from miles away - you may become the antidote for relationships ending only because of distance or the antidote for really awkward phone sex.

Likewise, when you come out in a community that may not welcome you, stand up for a friend who has a different sexual identity than you, or create a family on your own terms, you may become the antidote millions of people are looking for.

# I CAN SAVE LIVES

In Canada today, men who have had sex with men (MSM) are indefinitely prohibited to donate blood for transfusion purposes. Since most men that identify as gay sleep with other men, most gay men can't ever donate blood at a blood bank.

As part of my MBA, I wrote a paper on whether or not Canadian Blood Services (CBS) should re-evaluate their stance on MSM blood donations and what effect that decision would have on their customer (the recipient of a blood or blood product donation) and society as a whole. I looked back through history to uncover why the regulation was put in place and to provide rational for why it currently still exists. I saw how language was used to create heightened emotions and blurred battle lines throughout history, and how information sources were only partially used by both sides.

For example: according to the surveillance report used to support the current regulation, MSM have a high HIV exposure rate. However, according to the same report, so do heterosexual black man (higher than MSM in fact) and heterosexual men and women that live in Saskatchewan and Ontario. While I'll refrain from rehashing my paper (as exciting and enlightening as it was to write), I will say that there is much work to be done here.

I believe that blood screening procedures need to continue creating a high level of safety and assurance for the recipients. I also believe the donor base could increase substantially if screening criteria were based on donor behaviour, instead of creating further geographic, ethnic, or demographic based deferrals.

What some folks may not know is that the Canadian Blood Services Network Centre for Applied Development, based in Vancouver, BC, is the only lab in Canada that currently allows donors prohibited to donate blood through a CBS clinic to donate for research purposes. So technically gay men can donate blood right now, just not for transfusion purposes yet.

It is my hope that one day CBS will no longer need to create any large marketing campaigns encouraging people to donate blood in order to meet growing demand.

It is also my hope that if my Dad ever severely falls on the ski hill and needs some blood, I will be able to give it to him.

That if my Nana ever needs a hip replacement, I can provide the units of blood required to make that surgery a success.

That if my sister or fellow athlete ever requires cardiovascular surgery, I can give them my blood to help them get back up and racing again in no time.

And that if my Mom is ever in a serious car accident, I can donate to save her life.

I know that this will be possible.

As leaders in making this happen, we need to take what is possible and make it probable. And then take what is probable and make it our reality.

In short, we have work to do.

# OUR WORK

Being gay is still illegal in some communities.
Being caught performing homosexual activities is still punishable by death.
Publically supporting equal rights for the LGBT community can result in violence and blood shed.

Media and art portraying homosexual characters or images are banned in some places.
Parents still cover their children's eyes when two men are seen kissing.
Strangers still resort to violence or hateful slurs when two men are holding hands in the street.

Large corporations help fund marketing campaigns that encourage the restriction of marriage to only male-female partnerships.
Community groups advocate for boycotts of companies that support equality or queer rights.
Religious leaders still believe that homosexuality is a choice or a disease.

Gay kids commit suicide as a result of the bullying they face at school or online.
Gay kids end up on the street because of the lack of support they face at home. Gay kids are not educated on sexual and mental health concerns affecting the queer population.

Leaders in our communities remain silent about their sexuality.
Our queer family members face both equal and unique forms of discrimination and oppression.
We watch someone being bullied online and don't do anything about it.

This list could go on.
And that's the point.
The work of gay men and our allies is far from over.
We have a long road to travel in front of us.

The good news is that we are in this together.

somewhere over the rainbow, skies are blue.
and the dreams that you dare to dream
really do come true.

- the wizard of oz -

# I WANT TO LOVE YOU UNCONDITIONALLY

Unconditional love is not:
"If you do, be, or say this, *then* I will love you."

That is conditional love.

There is a requirement there that one must meet in order to receive your love.

Unconditional love is free from those requirements, standards or expectations.

It is:
I love you and everything that makes you you.

I love the awkward, the hilarious, the endearing and the hard to understand parts of you.

I want to know you more so that I can love you more.

Unconditional love is "I love you."

Period.

what if I loved myself
unconditionally?

# THE FINAL BREATH

What if this was the last conversation you ever had with him?

What if you died tomorrow and that conversation became your final words?

What would you want to end your conversation with?

Try: I love you.

it all works out in the end. and if it hasn't
worked out yet, then it isn't the end.

# a moment of clarity

## reflect

→ What does faith mean to you? Where does faith show up in your life?

→ What name do you use when describing the force that looks out for you and the people you love?

→ What have you overcome in your life that you could now help someone else overcome?

→ How can you help someone else on their journey? What would you tell some one who is struggling?

→ Who can you offer unconditional love to so that it would transform the relationship you have with them?

→ What legacy do you want to leave in this world? What do you need to do this week to become one step closer towards that legacy?

→ What one unlikely and highly remarkable event will completely blow your mind when it happens in the future?

## action

1) Go to and sit silently in a sacred space - be it a quiet corner of your room or a temple of some sort. What do you experience while being silent in this place?

_____

_____

_____

_____

_____

_____

_____

_____

_____

2) List out three examples of beings you would consider to be enlightened. What qualities do they possess that you would also like to embody?

**PERSON #1:**

_____

_____

_____

_____

_____

_____

**PERSON #2:**

_____

_____

_____

_____

_____

_____

**PERSON #3:**

_____

_____

_____

_____

_____

_____

3) Describe yourself and your world when you are 80-years-old. Be as specific as possible. After you have done that, write a letter from your 80-year-old self to you today. What advice would your 80-year-old self give to you?

4) Get involved in a community or organization that is supporting a cause you feel passionate about. Be part of the change.

# WHEN WE GET OVER THE RAINBOW

We take a journey towards our fullest self expression.
We follow a pathway created for us to find our happy ending.
We look inside ourselves to uncover the pot of gold we were searching for.

When we get over the rainbow...
We break through the perceived and real barriers that hold us back.
We envision and create a future we want to move towards.
We take action to move towards it.

When we get over the rainbow...
We embrace the stereotypes and queer icons for all that they are and the history they represent.
We take each hateful word and punch to the gut with grace and forgiveness.
We step out of the shadows and into the light.

When we get over the rainbow..
We live a full and vibrant life that radiates with love.
We make a difference in the lives of those around us.
We make a difference in our own life.

When we get over the rainbow...
We create something remarkable.
We become someone remarkable.

When we get over the rainbow...
We create a movement.

When we get over the rainbow...
We become the movement.

# THIS ISN'T THE END

The chapters end here.
That doesn't mean, however, that the conversations or journey has to.

Maybe you share this book with someone you love.
Maybe you rip out a page and post it on your fridge.
Maybe you pick up a pen and begin writing the book that will fill in all the gaps this one leaves.

Or maybe you pick up the phone and call him.
And tell him that you love him.

Because at the end of it all, I really want you to love him. All of him.
And I also really want you to love yourself. All of that too.

It's that kind of unconditional love that will last forever.

Namaste.

# TO MY BIGGEST FANS

My heart explodes with gratitude and love for all the people that made this book possible. To say I am "thankful" is like calling a mighty oak tree "tall" or the ocean "damp." The magnitude of my gratefulness can not be accurately captured in a few words. But here I go anyway...

To Mom and Dad - thank you for all your perfect mistakes and your amazing acts of love throughout the years. I am blessed to have such great examples like you in my life.

To my sis - I adore us. I adore our adventures, our sweat sessions, and our unwavering support of one another. Thank you for always being a reminder of what playing really big means.

To Haas - you redefine how to be a best friend. Thank you DHB.

To Felicia, Ange, Adam, and Zoe - I appreciate that you have pushed me to write, to read, to articulate my thoughts, and to go after my big goals. Thank you for always seeing the best in me.

To Joe & Peter - your love is an absolute light in my life. Thank you for being so generous with it.

To Darryl, Darran, Andrew, Steve, Carlson, Jack, Conor, Rob, and Josh - your friendship means the world to me. Nay, the cosmos! Thank you for being part of the gaggle who provided many great dance parties, deep chats, and tough love. I am a better man because of you.

To Kai - thank you for sharing your journey with me. This book would not have existed if not for your honesty and your willingness to be vulnerable. How's that for your legacy!

To Josh and Lauren - you created spaces for me to get away to and dive deep in to my writing. Our laughs and delicious meals together were the perfect balance to my pen and paper.

To Katie - you are the best goal champion a writer could ever ask for. Thank you for your faith in me and in this book.

To Emma - you make dreams beautiful. Thank you for creating such a masterpiece and smiling through all my neurotic edits along the way.

To all the writers and editors that read, edited, and ripped apart the initial drafts - thank you for treating my baby with the tough love it needed to be what it is today.

To my ex-boyfriends, the archetypes, my one night stands, the Mermates, my yoga teachers and kula across the sea, my professors, mentors, and coaches - thank you for providing the perfect backdrop and playing ground for all the lessons I needed to learn.

To God - thank you for all your blessings. Even the ones that didn't appear that way at the time.

To you, the reader - thank you for reading this.
I hope it made you smile as big as typing this last line made me.

## ABOUT MATT CORKER

I once thought that I wasn't good enough because I am gay. I focused on proving myself and the value I brought by being the best at whatever I was doing. That way no one could discount the difference I was making because of my sexual orientation.

Then, one day I accidentally wore my new boyfriend's shoes out to brunch with my sister. From then on, I discovered how amazing life can be when living life to make a difference rather to impress.

Now, I love who I am.
Now, I'm part of an incredible family and community. Now, I feel fulfilled in how I contribute to the world.

And I wish the same for you.

 To learn more about me, stop by
www.mattcorker.com

49575256R00086

Made in the USA
Charleston, SC
29 November 2015